The Gift

Christmas
Luke Chapters 1 & 2

Jeffrey D. Johnson

Wipf & Stock
PUBLISHERS
Eugene, Oregon

Wipf and Stock Publishers
199 W 8th Ave, Suite 3
Eugene, OR 97401

The Gift
Christmas: Luke 1 & 2
By Johnson, Jeffrey D.

ISBN 13: 978-1-55635-082-5
ISBN 10: 1-55635-082-1
Publication date 11/30/2006

About Israel Today Ministries

Three-fold Purpose:

- Teach the Church about Israel
- Teach Israel about their Messiah
- Help feed those in need (Romans 15:27; Genesis 12:1-3)

To receive Dr. Johnson's "teaching letters," or, if you would like to send a gift to Israel Today Ministries, or if you would like Dr. Johnson to speak at your church event, school, or small group, contact:

Israel Today Ministries
P.O. Box 150288
Arlington, TX 76015
Phone/Fax 817.468.4441
E mail: Galileeman@juno.com

This is Yossef (Joseph) and Abigail. Your monthly donations help feed little ones like these.

"Inasmuch as ye have done it unto one of the least of these my brethren, ye have done it unto me" –Jesus, Matthew 25:40

About Dr. Jeffrey D. Johnson

- Three decades in ministry
- Founder/Director of Israel Today Ministries
- Director of tours to the Middle East
- Senior pastor in Ohio, Massachusetts and California
- Almost 7 years directorship with International Ministries to Israel (formerly, The American Association for Jewish Evangelism, where the famed Hyman Appelman was the first president)
- Conference speaker
- Bible expositor
- Guest lecturer
- Author

Born and raised in the Midwest, Dr. Johnson took his B.D. from Massillon Baptist College, his MA from Moody Bible Institute, and his Th.M. and Th.D. from Christian Bible College. His passion for Israel, the Jewish roots of Christianity and Bible prophecy, is well known. His teaching will stir your heart to follow the Lord and to love and *"pray for the peace of Jerusalem"* (Psalm 122:6).

As an "Itinerant Bible Teacher," Dr. Johnson will travel anywhere to proclaim God's redeeming Grace through our Lord and Savior Jesus the Messiah, *"to the Jew first, and also to the Greek"* (Romans 1:16).

His call is to *"Teach the Church about Israel; Teach Israel about their Messiah; and to feed those in need"* (Genesis 12:3; Romans 15:27).

Dr. Jeff and his wife, Louise, have purposed to serve the Lord trusting God to provide the funds and resources for their livelihood.

Israel Today Ministries, founded by Dr. Johnson, is a faith ministry, supported by "love offerings" from those desiring to bless Israel. Dr. Jeff and Louise have been commissioned and sent out by their home church.

Comments from Christian Leaders

I am pleased to recommend him to churches as an able expositor of the Word of God.

– *the late* **John Walvoord**, Chancellor,
Dallas Theological Seminary

A Bible Expositor with special insights on the origin, nature and destiny of God's chosen people, Israel.

– **John C. Whitcomb**, Bible Scholar, Author, Professor

A careful expositor of Scripture.

– **Homer Kent**, President Emeritus,
Grace College and Seminary

A practitioner of all that he preaches.

– **Paige Patterson**, former President of the
Southern Baptist Convention, President,
Southeastern Baptist Theological Seminary

He has a wonderful grasp of Jewish history and liturgy.

– **Edgar C. James**, Professor, Moody Bible Institute

He is a person who has been uniquely prepared by God to preach and teach about God's special people. Any one who hears him will come away with a great love for the people of Abraham.

–**Dick Dahlquist**, Chair, Pastoral Studies, Acting Dean,
Grace College of Graduate Studies

He has a gifted teaching ministry which encompasses Biblical prophecy and insights into modern-day Judaism.

–the late **Paul Tassell**, Bible Scholar, Author,
former National Representative of the G.A.R.B.C.

He has a great ministry.

– **LaVerne Butler**, former President of Mid-Continent Baptist College, Scholar, Conference Speaker, President, Pulpit Aflame

Your heart will be thrilled as he ministers the prophetic Scriptures.

– the late **Alden A. Gannett**, President Emeritus of Southeastern Bible College, Bible Scholar, Author, Conference Speaker, President, Gannett Ministries

He loves the people and nation of Israel. He has given himself to a thorough study of God's ancient people and of the prophetic.

– **Ivan H. French**, Pastor Emeritus, Pleasant View Bible Church, former Professor, Grace College and Seminary

Christmas

"A little girl came home from Sunday school triumphantly waving a paper. 'Mommy!' she said. 'My teacher says I drew the most unusual Christmas picture she has ever seen!' The mother studied the picture for a moment and concluded it was indeed a very peculiar Christmas picture. 'This is wonderfully drawn, but why have you made all these people riding on the back of an airplane?' the mother gently asked. 'It's the flight into Egypt,' the little girl said, with a hint of disappointment that the picture's meaning was not immediately obvious. 'Oh,' the mother said cautiously. 'Well, who is the mean-looking man at the front?' 'That's Pontius, the Pilot,' the girl said, now visibly impatient. 'I see. And here you have Mary and Joseph and the baby,' the mother volunteered. Studying the picture silently for a moment, she summoned the courage to ask, 'But who is this (heavy) man sitting behind Mary?' The little girl sighed. 'Can't you tell? That's Round John Virgin!'"[1]

We laugh, but indeed the true meaning of Christmas has been lost in the midst of legend, ignorance, and commercialism. It is easy to forget the purpose and meaning of this most important day.

In eons past, in the Eternal Mind of God, our loving Lord created the world, the planets, the stars…the universe…so that the pinnacle of His creation, namely man, could understand a little bit of the glory of the Creator. God communed with man in the Garden and after the Fall. He communicated to Noah, Abraham, Isaac, and Jacob and then through the prophets, priests and kings. God communicated a story of an Anointed One that would come. The Messiah of Israel and the world. A Messiah that would become a sacrificial Lamb and ultimately become the Lion of Judah, the King of Kings.

This hope struck a vein deep within the Jewish soul and moved this oppressed and conquered people with a passion of wonder as to when will the Anointed One come. It has been nearly 400 years since God directly communicated through a prophet. Rome's powerful arm of oppression embraced the known world. And every Jewish girl, since the time of Abraham, wonders if she will be the one chosen, through whom Messiah will come. Hope is waning as four centuries have come and gone and no message from God. Until now…

Luke One

"There was in the days of Herod, the king of Judaea, a certain priest named Zacharias, of the course of Abia: and his wife was of the daughters of Aaron, and her name was Elisabeth. And they were both righteous before God, walking in all the commandments and ordinances of the Lord blameless. And they had no child, because that Elisabeth was barren, and they both were now well stricken in years. And it came to pass, that while he executed the priest's office before God in the order of his course, According to

the custom of the priest's office, his lot was to burn incense when he went into the temple of the Lord. And the whole multitude of the people were praying without at the time of incense. And there appeared unto him an angel of the Lord standing on the right side of the altar of incense. And when Zacharias saw him, he was troubled, and fear fell upon him. But the angel said unto him, Fear not, Zacharias: for thy prayer is heard; and thy wife Elisabeth shall bear thee a son, and thou shalt call his name John. And thou shalt have joy and gladness; and many shall rejoice at his birth. For he shall be great in the sight of the Lord, and shall drink neither wine nor strong drink; and he shall be filled with the Holy Ghost, even from his mother's womb. And many of the children of Israel shall he turn to the Lord their God. And he shall go before him in the spirit and power of Elias, to turn the hearts of the fathers to the children, and the disobedient to the wisdom of the just; to make ready a people prepared for the Lord. And Zacharias said unto the angel, whereby shall I know this? For I am an old man, and my wife well stricken in years. And the angel answering said unto him, I am Gabriel, that stand in the presence of God; and am sent to speak unto thee, and to shew thee these glad tidings. And, behold, thou shalt be dumb, and not able to speak, until the day that these things shall be performed, because thou believest not my words, which shall be fulfilled in their season. And the people waited for Zacharias, and marvelled that he tarried so long in the temple. And when he came out, he could not speak unto them: and they perceived that he had seen a vision in the temple: for he beckoned unto them, and remained speechless. And it came to pass, that, as soon as the days of his ministration were accomplished, he departed to his own house. And after those days his wife Elisabeth conceived, and hid herself five months, saying, thus hath the Lord dealt with me in the days wherein he looked on me, to take away my reproach among men." Luke 1:5-25

John's birth is announced to Zacharias, a priest of the temple. Elizabeth, his wife, will give birth to John the Baptist, who will be the one crying in the wilderness, the one prophesied of old, having the spirit and power of Elijah, preparing the way for the Lord.

Verses 26-38: Messiah's birth announced to Mary.

"And in the sixth month the angel Gabriel was sent from God unto a city of Galilee, named Nazareth, To a virgin espoused to a man whose name was Joseph, of the house of David; and the virgin's name was Mary. And the angel came in unto her, and said, Hail, thou that art highly favoured, the Lord is with thee: blessed art thou among women. And when she saw him, she was troubled at his saying, and cast in her mind what manner of salutation this should be. And the angel said unto her, Fear not, Mary: for thou hast found favour with God. And, behold, thou shalt conceive in thy womb, and bring forth a son, and shalt call his name JESUS. He shall be great, and shall be called the Son of the Highest: and the Lord God shall give unto him the throne of his father David: and he shall reign over the house of Jacob for ever; and of his kingdom there shall be no end. Then said Mary unto the angel, How shall this be, seeing I know not a man? And the angel answered and said unto her, The Holy Ghost shall come upon thee, and the power of the Highest shall overshadow thee: therefore also that holy thing which shall be born of thee shall be called the Son of God. And, behold, thy cousin Elisabeth, she hath also conceived a son in her old age: and this is the sixth month with her, who was called barren. For with God nothing shall be impossible. And Mary said, Behold the handmaid of the Lord; be it unto me according to thy word. And the angel departed from her." Luke1: 26-38

Verse 35: The angel's response is a Hebraic expression of "sublime sentiment and poetical style. The angel…deals with one of the deepest and holiest mysteries, and for this reason his words are here exalted to a song. In a tender and chaste manner, he declares in the song the fact of the impending pregnancy of the Virgin Mary through divine influence. The Holy Spirit will come upon Mary and overshadow her with His power, through which she will become pregnant.

In the original Greek…(the reference is) to the creative operation or power (of the Holy Spirit). The 'power of the Highest' is thus used as synonymous with it. Like a cloud, the symbol of the divine presence in which God appears, the power of the Highest shall overshadow her."[2]

"…And the spirit of God moved upon the face of the waters."
Genesis 1:2

"And Mary arose in those days, and went into the hill country with haste, into a city of Juda; And entered into the house of Zacharias, and saluted Elisabeth. And it came to pass, that, when Elisabeth heard the salutation of Mary, the babe leaped in her womb; and Elisabeth was filled with the Holy Ghost: and she spake out with a loud voice, and said, blessed art thou among women, and blessed is the fruit of thy womb. And whence is this to me, that the mother of my Lord should come to me? For, lo, as soon as the voice of thy salutation sounded in mine ears, the babe leaped in my womb for joy. And blessed is she that believed: for there shall be a performance of those things which were told her from the Lord." Luke 1:39-45

Verses 39-45: Mary visits Elizabeth

"Luke has incorporated in his gospel three complete hymns used by the early Christians, the Magnificat, the Song of Mary (Luke 1:46-55); the Benedictus, the Song of

Zacharias (Luke 1:68-79); and Nunc Dimittis, the Song of Simeon (Luke 2:29-32); each known from the opening words of the Latin Vulgate."[3]

Luke Two

It is written in Haggai that God says, *"I will shake heaven and earth, the sea and dry land; and I will shake all nations, and they shall come to the Desire of All Nations…" Haggai 2:6,7*

Verses 1-3: "And it came to pass in those days, that there went out a decree from Caesar Augustus, that all the world should be taxed. (And this taxing was first made when Cyrenius was governor of Syria.) And all went to be taxed, every one into his own city."

"In those days"

"Caesar Augustus was the first Roman emperor. His real name was Caius Octavius. He was a great-nephew of Julius Caesar. The word Augustus is significant. That was his title. He took the name Caesar by courtesy and by adoption."[4] In time the title Augustus was dropped and the title became Caesar. It was a time of the famous "Pax Romana", so called Roman Peace. This was a time when the Roman Republic became the Roman Empire when the Romans were under an autocratic ruler. This autocratic ruler and empire "had bludgeoned the world into submission…the whole world was crushed under (his) heel."[5]

"Interestingly, a petition for tax relief from the Jews to Caesar Augustus delayed the census for a period of time so that Mary came full term while they were still in Bethlehem."[6]

Verses 4,5: "And Joseph also went up from Galilee, out of the city of Nazareth, into Judaea, unto the city of David, which is called Bethlehem; (because he was of the house and lineage of David:) To be taxed with Mary his espoused wife, being great with child."

"Joseph, who was of the house of David, had to go to Bethlehem. Here David had been born a thousand years previously. Originally the town had been called Efratha (Genesis 35:19)."[7] Joseph and Mary, were only two people amid the multitudes that were now in the region. Only two people amid the masses of the Roman Empire. They had no more effect on Caesar Augustus and the Roman Empire than any two of us would have on the President of the United States. Joseph "went up, and Mary traveled with him; two people. Nobody knew about it, except perhaps the friends of Mary and of Joseph and they did not know much about it.

But look again. Two individuals marching under the orders of Caesar Augustus. Look at the woman. Her womb is the tabernacle of the Son of God as she travels. Look at the man. The one passion of his life is to guard that woman."[8]

The way traveled from Nazareth would have been long and weary. It would have taken them at least three days journey. They probably came the commonly traveled route along the eastern banks of the Jordan, then through Jericho. This was the warmest part of the country. It would have been very difficult. "A sense of rest and peace…crept over the travelers when at last they reached the rich fields that surrounded the ancient 'House of Bread', …passing through the valley which, like an amphitheater, sweeps up to the (two) heights along which Bethlehem stretches, ascending through the terraced vineyards and gardens."[9] Perhaps they recalled the stories of Ruth and Boaz, Jesse and David.

"That edict of Caesar Augustus rippled across the world, touching everyone. Even Joseph and Mary must go."[10]

But something greater than this unfolded. A prophecy was written at least 650 years before. In Micah we read:

"But thou, Bethlehem Ephratah, though thou be little among the thousands of Judah, yet out of thee shall he come forth unto me that is to be ruler in Israel; whose goings forth have been from of old, from everlasting." Micah 5:2

"When I read that, uttered 650 years before these events, I see that the really insignificant person in the drama is the little puppet (in Rome) called Caesar Augustus; and the significant personalities are the woman in whose womb tabernacles the Son of God, and the man who is guarding her."[11]

Verses 6, 7: "And so it was, that, while they were there, the days were accomplished that she should be delivered. And she brought forth her firstborn son, and wrapped him in swaddling clothes, and laid him in a manger; because there was no room for them in the inn."

"No room for them in the inn".

Martin Luther stated that Mary and Joseph "were the most insignificant and despised, so that they had to make way for others until they were obliged to take refuge in a stable, to share with the cattle lodging, table, bedchamber and bed, while many a wicked man sat at the head in the hotels and was honored as lord. No one noticed or was conscious of what God was doing in that stable…O what a dark night this was for Bethlehem, that was not conscious of that glorious light!"[12]

"Although Mary's critical situation was clear to all, no one gave up accommodation to her and Joseph.... The early church father, Justin Martyr (A.D.150), states that this 'stable' was a cave. About A.D. 330, Constantine...caused a church to be built over this cave."[13] (This church still has services; it is the oldest practicing church.)

The area of this cave was used for bazaars and markets, where animals were killed, and meat sold there...a place for wine and cider to be stored so in fact it was a more public place than we would imagine. People were walking to and fro. Mary would have been in view of the public at large.

"He was born outside everything. Passed the court, passed the palace, passed the inn, passed the dwelling place...and was born into this world so low...that no baby could ever be born lower."[14]

"She brought forth her firstborn Son, and wrapped Him in swaddling clothes."

"It is very beautiful, but oh, the pity of it, the tragedy of it, the loneliness of it; that in that hour of all hours, when a (woman) should be surrounded by the tenderest care, she was alone. The method of the writer is very distinct. She with her own hands wrapped the Baby round with those swaddling clothes, and laid Him in the manger. There was no one to do it for her."[15] "The swaddling clothes, it is said, are used for grave clothes. Possibly, her veil or some article of (Mary's) clothing she could spare."[16]

This Anointed One, foretold, was born that night...

Notice the words "firstborn Son". "The simple meaning is that Jesus was her eldest Child, the first born Son. But there is a larger meaning. Firstborn does not mean only first in time, it means also first in place, first in order, first in importance. In the New Testament He is called, 'Firstborn of creation'. He is called 'Firstborn from the dead'. He is called 'Firstborn of many brethren'...(and yet there is a more profound note). Who is this child? The Son of God.

That is what happened in that manger. There in that little town of Bethlehem Ephratah, the Son of God, in human form, had entered the stream of human history."[17]

Verse 8: *Shepherds. "And there were in the same country shepherds abiding in the field, keeping watch over their flock by night."*

"Somewhere in the fields near Bethlehem, where David many centuries before had also kept sheep, a small group of shepherds were keeping watch over their sheep."[18]

These were not ordinary shepherds. These shepherds watch the flocks destined for sacrificial services near the place consecrated and foretold by the prophet that the Messiah would be revealed.

Verse 9: *Angel, Glory of the Lord "And, lo, the angel of the Lord came upon them, and the glory of the Lord shone round about them: and they were sore afraid."*

Rabbinical tradition states that "wherever Michael appears, there also is the glory of the Shekhinah."[19] "The glory of the Lord seemed to enwrap them, as in a mantle of light."[20] "The radiating glory of God's majesty became visible to them as it had appeared to Moses at the burning bush, to the Israelites in the pillar of fire in the desert…to the worshippers in the tabernacle or temple, or as it would later in becoming visible to the three disciples on the Mountain of Transfiguration."[21]

Verses 10-12: The Message *"And the angel said unto them, Fear not: for, behold, I bring you good tidings of great joy, which shall be to all people. For unto you is born this day in the city of David a Saviour, which is Christ the Lord. And this shall be a sign unto you; Ye shall find the babe wrapped in swaddling clothes, lying in a manger."*

Before the shepherds could respond or say a word…

Verses 13,14: *"And suddenly there was with the angel a multitude of the heavenly host praising God, and saying, Glory to God in the highest and on earth peace, good will toward men."*

Only once before had the words of the angels' hymn fallen upon (man's) ears, when Isaiah: "saw the Lord sitting on a throne, high and lifted up, and the train of His robe filled the temple…(and he heard the angelic host crying) Holy, holy, holy is the Lord of Hosts; the whole earth is full of His glory."

Verse 15a: *Angels had gone away. "And it came to pass, as the angels were gone away from them into heaven…"*

"The host of angels had appeared unexpectedly and suddenly, but (as indicated by the Greek) they departed gradually so that the shepherds could see them ascending to heaven. By this means they could better realize the actuality of what had happened…As a result, there is no question of doubt with them concerning the truth of the tidings brought by the (angel). They know that the event has actually taken place and realize that it is the Lord who has sent them the (good news) through the angel."[22]

Verse 15-20: *"…the shepherds said one to another, Let us now go even unto Bethlehem, and see this thing which is come to pass, which the Lord hath made known unto us. And they came with haste, and found Mary, and Joseph, and the babe lying in a manger. And when they had seen it, they made known abroad the saying which was told them concerning this child. And all they that heard it wondered at those things which were told them by the shepherds. But Mary kept all these things, and pondered them in her heart. And the shepherds returned, glorifying and praising God for all the things that they had heard and seen, as it was told unto them."*

"The Magi (wise men), who would come much later, had a star to guide them. But all the shepherds had was the sign given them by the angels."[23] It took much time and effort to find the Christ Child.

Shepherding was the lowest of vocations at this time. They were on the lowest rung of society. Luther made this comment about the shepherds. "How very richly God honors those who are despised of men…Here you see that His eyes look into the depths of humility, as is written, 'He sitteth above the cherubim' and looketh into the depths. Nor could the angels find princes or valiant men to whom to communicate the good news; but only unlearned laymen, the most humble people on earth. Could they not have addressed the high priest, who was supposed (to know) so much concerning God and the angels? No, God chose poor shepherds, who, though they were of low esteem in the sight of men, were in heaven regarded as worthy of such great grace and honor."[24] These humble shepherds saw with their own eyes the Promised One of Old.

They made "widely known" these events throughout Jerusalem and vicinity. Anna and Simeon probably heard through the shepherds the glorious news of the Christ Child. Masses of people began to wonder about this strange and wonderful story. Could it be? Has He come? Has Isaiah's prophecy come true?

"For unto us a child is born, Unto us a Son is given (?)."
Isaiah 9:6

"To Us, to Us, to Us is born and to Us is given this Child."[25]

"For God so loved the world that He gave His only begotten Son, that whosoever believeth in him should not perish, but have everlasting life." John 3:16

This One, this Anointed One of Old, foretold by the prophets, came 2000 years ago, born of a Virgin. In the "fullness of time" the "Morning Star" appeared, the Eternal Son of God. God tabernacled in the flesh. As Mary kissed the brow of her baby boy, she was in fact, kissing the very face of God.

How will you respond to this message? Will you, like the "inhabitants of Bethlehem did in…ignorance…(and like) many today in willful indifference…refuse to make room for the Son of God (?)…to give no place to Him in their feelings, their affections, their thoughts, their views of life, their wishes, their decisions, their actions, or their daily conduct. And thus deny themselves the greatest privilege of all and incur the greatest loss to their lives (?)."[26]

Paul wrote, *"Thanks be to God for His indescribable gift!" 2 Corinthians 9:15*

This gift is His Son, the Messiah, the Anointed One, the Savior.

"He that believeth on the Son hath everlasting life: and he that believeth not the Son shall not see life; but the wrath of God abideth on him." John 3:36

Jesus said, *"...I am the light of the world: he that followeth me shall not walk in darkness, but shall have the light of life." John 8:12*

The greatest gift you can receive this Christmas, is the gift of eternal life through Jesus Christ our Lord. If you have never received Him as Saviour...like the shepherds please come with haste; come quickly to see the Son of God. He is a free gift to you from the Heavenly Father.

Christian, let our main focus this Christmas be upon God's gift to us and may we like Mary treasure all these things and ponder them in our hearts.

"For God so loved the world that He gave H is only begotten Son..."

And Jesus gave His all for us, though He being God...

"made Himself of no reputation, taking the form of a bondservant, and coming in the likeness of men (so that we would understand)...humbled Himself and became obedient to ...death, even the death of the cross." Philippians 2:7-8 NKJV (and He rose on the third day)

"How else can we respond (to this?) But by giving ourselves to Him completely in return."[27] Come...and receive the Gift.

Endnotes

[1] John F. MacArthur, Jr., *"God With Us, The Miracle of Christmas"*, (Zondervan Publishing House, Grand Rapids, Michigan, 1989), pp. 13,14.
[2] Norval Geldenhuys, *"The New International Commentary on the New Testament, The Gospel of Luke"*, (Wm. B. Eerdmans Publishing Company, Grand Rapids, Michigan, 1979), pp. 76, 77.
[3] Ernest Fremont Tittle, *"The Gospel According to Luke"*, (Harper & Brothers Publishers, New York 1951), p. 5.
[4] G. Campbell Morgan, *"The Gospel According to Luke"*, (Fleming H. Revell Company, 1931), p. 34.
[5] Ibid., p. 34.
[6] Moishe Rosen, *"Y'Shua"*, (Moody Press, Chicago, 1982), p. 13.
[7] Norval Geldenhuys, *"The International Commentary on the New Testament, The Gospel of Luke"*, (Wm. B. Eerdmans Publishing Company, Grand Rapids, Michigan, 1979), p. 100.
[8] G. Campbell Morgan, *"The Gospel According to Luke"*, (Fleming H. Revell Company, 1931), p. 35.
[9] Alfred Edersheim, *"The Life and Times of Jesus the Messiah, Volume One"*, (Wm. B. Eerdmans Publishing Co., Grand Rapids, Michigan, Photolithoprinted, 1965), p. 184.
[10] G. Campbell Morgan, *"The Gospel According to Luke"*, (Fleming H. Revell Company, 1931), p. 35.
[11] Ibid., p. 35.
[12] Calvin Miller, *"The Book of Jesus"*, (Simon & Schuster, New York 1996), p. 121.
[13] Norval Geldenhuys, *"The International Commentary on the New Testament, The Gospel of Luke"*, (Wm. B. Eerdmans Publishing Company, Grand Rapids, Michigan, 1979), p. 101.
[14] G. Campbell Morgan, *"The Gospel According to Luke"*, (Fleming H. Revell Company, 1931), p. 36.
[15] Ibid., p. 36.
[16] Calvin Miller, *"The Book of Jesus"*, (Simon & Schuster, New York, 1996), p. 121.

[17] G. Campbell Morgan, *"The Gospel According to Luke"*, (Fleming H. Revell Company, 1931), p. 36.
[18] Norval Geldenhuys, *"The International Commentary on the New Testament, The Gospel of Luke"*, (Wm. B. Eerdmans Publishing Company, Grand Rapids, Michigan, 1979), p. 111.
[19] Alfred Edersheim, *"The Life and Times of Jesus the Messiah, Volume One"*, (Wm. B. Eerdmans Publishing Co., Grand Rapids, Michigan, Photolithoprinted, 1965), p. 187.
[20] Ibid., p. 187.
[21] Norval Geldenhuys, *"The International Commentary on the New Testament, The Gospel of Luke"*, (Wm. B. Eerdmans Publishing Company, Grand Rapids, Michigan, 1979), p. 111.
[22] Ibid., p. 187.
[23] Warren W. Wiersbe, *"Wiersbe's Expository Outlines on the New Testament"*, (Victor Books, 1992), p. 151.
[24] Calvin Miller, *"The Book of Jesus"*, (Simon & Schuster, New York, 1996), p. 122,123.
[25] Ibid., p. 123.
[26] Norval Geldenhuys, *"The International Commentary on the New Testament, The Gospel of Luke"*, (Wm. B. Eerdmans Publishing Company, Grand Rapids, Michigan, 1979), p. 102.
[27] John F. MacArthur, Jr., *"God With Us, The Miracle of Christmas"*, (Zondervan Publishing House, Grand Rapids, Michigan, 1989), p. 134.